THE UNEXPLAINED

ALIEN ABDUCTIONS

BY JUSTIN ERICKSON

TORQUE™

BELLWETHER MEDIA • MINNEAPOLIS, MN

Are you ready to take it to the extreme?
Torque books thrust you into the action-packed world
of sports, vehicles, mystery, and adventure. These books
may include dirt, smoke, fire, and dangerous stunts.
WARNING : read at your own risk.

Library of Congress Cataloging-in-Publication Data

Erickson, Justin.
 Alien abductions / by Justin Erickson.
    p. cm. -- (Torque: the unexplained)
 Summary: "Engaging images accompany information about alien abductions.
The combination of high-interest subject matter and light text is intended for students in grades 3
through 7"--Provided by publisher.
Includes bibliographical references and index.
 ISBN 978-1-60014-582-7 (hardcover : alk. paper)
 1. Human-alien encounters-- Juvenile literature. I. Title.
 BF2050.E75 2011
 001.942--dc22   2010034773

This edition first published in 2011 by Bellwether Media, Inc.

Printed in the United States of America, North Mankato, MN.

010111   1176

CONTENTS

CHAPTER 1
ABOARD AN ALIEN SPACECRAFT

Betty and Barney Hill were driving down an empty road in New Hampshire on September 19, 1961. They noticed a strange light following them in the sky. Betty told Barney to pull over. They got out to look at the light through binoculars. Betty thought it looked like a **satellite** or a spacecraft. Barney thought it was just an airplane. They got back into their car and kept driving.

Betty and Barney Hill

Suddenly, the bright light landed in front of them. Barney thought it looked like a spacecraft with **aliens** inside. The couple became light-headed and lost track of the next several hours. In the morning, they had memories of being aboard an alien spacecraft. They also noticed their clothes were torn.

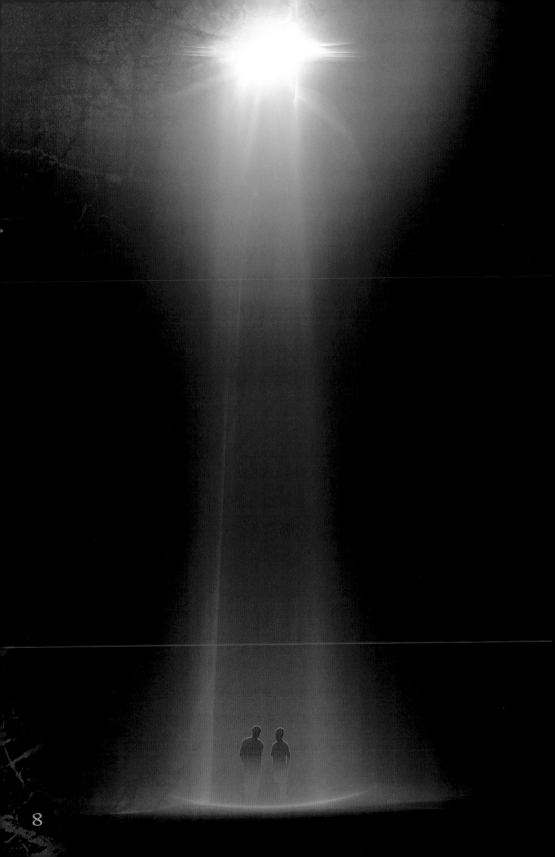

Many people think the Hills made this story up to become famous. They claim it is a **hoax**. Others believe that the Hills were truly **abducted** by aliens.

THE GRAYS

The Hills reported that the aliens they saw were gray and had large, triangular heads. They also said the aliens had big, dark eyes and small mouths. Many people call these aliens "The Grays."

CHAPTER 2
WHAT ARE ALIEN ABDUCTIONS?

People all around the world have claimed they were abducted by aliens. Most reported abductions last no longer than a few days. Many people describe seeing a bright light in the sky. They recall being taken aboard an alien spacecraft. Some people report going through painful medical tests. Others claim aliens tried to read their minds.

Not all abduction victims report bad experiences. Some victims say aliens just talked with them. These people claim they received warnings about the effects of **pollution** and the dangers of nuclear weapons.

TRACKING DEVICES

A few abduction victims claim that aliens placed small pieces of metal inside of them. Many people think these metal objects track the movement of the victims on Earth.

FAMOUS ABDUCTIONS

Year	Place
1961	New Hampshire
1967	Nebraska
1973	Mississippi
1975	Arizona
1985	Scotland
1985	New York
1993	California
1997	Russia

Incident

Betty and Barney Hill claim they were abducted by aliens. This abduction report is the first to be in news stories across the country.

Police officer Herbert Schirmer reports being abducted by reptile-like aliens.

Two fishermen report being paralyzed and taken aboard an alien spacecraft. Both men take a lie detector test. The tests show they are telling the truth.

Logger Travis Walton goes missing for five days. He is found looking thin and unshaven. He claims that he was held by aliens resembling the Grays.

Forester Robert Taylor reports seeing an alien spacecraft. He says he fell unconscious and woke up feeling confused.

Author Whitley Strieber is awakened by a strange creature in his bedroom. Later, under hypnosis, he speaks of boarding an alien spacecraft. His tale becomes famous in a book and movie titled *Communion*.

Dr. Roger Leir removes three metal objects from the bodies of two patients. The patients claim to have been abducted by aliens.

Kirsan Ilyumzhinov, the future President of the Russian Republic of Kalmykia, claims he was abducted from his apartment and taken aboard an alien spacecraft.

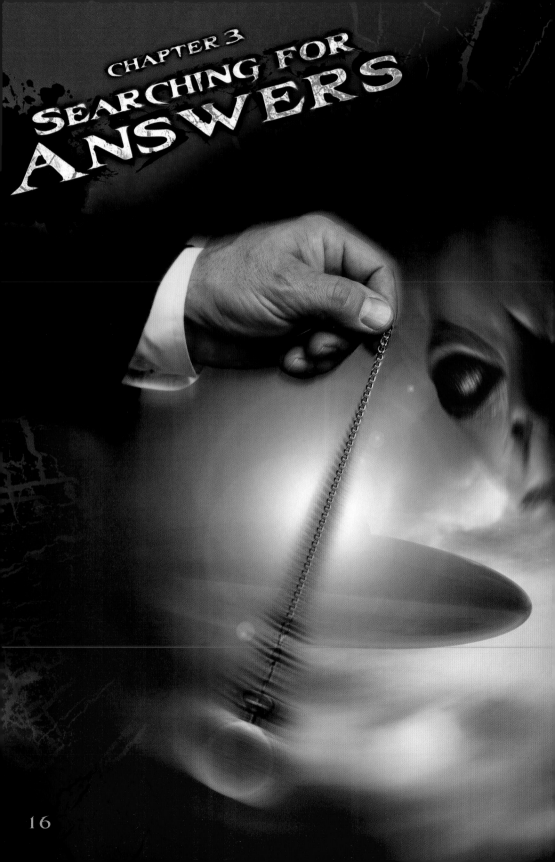

CHAPTER 3
SEARCHING FOR ANSWERS

Is there any proof that alien abductions really happen? Some people point to the small pieces of metal removed from victims as proof. They also point to the memory loss and torn clothes that victims often report. Some look to **hypnosis** for proof. People who are hypnotized often recall more details about their abductions.

Dr. Roger Leir

Dr. Roger Leir wrote *The Aliens and the Scalpel* about his operations on abduction victims.

Many **theories** try to explain why aliens would take people from Earth. One theory is that the Grays are old and dying. They want human **genes** to help them survive. Others believe that the Grays are observing Earth and studying humans. They might want to prepare for an attack.

MOO-VING ON UP?

People might not be the only beings aliens are abducting. Some people think that aliens are also taking cows.

20

Skeptics believe that all abduction stories are hoaxes. They think people make the stories up to get into the news. Many think abduction stories are just vivid dreams.

We have little to worry about if the skeptics are right. However, if they are wrong, we should watch out for bright lights in the night sky!

GLOSSARY

abducted—kidnapped

aliens—beings from other planets

genes—small bits of information within living cells; genes determine a living being's traits.

hoax—an attempt to trick people into believing something

hypnosis—a state of extreme relaxation that often allows one's mind to recall things it cannot in a conscious state

pollution—damage to Earth's environment caused by harmful materials

satellite—an object placed into orbit high above Earth for communication purposes

skeptics—people who do not believe in something

theories—ideas that try to explain why something exists or happens

TO LEARN MORE

AT THE LIBRARY

Helstrom, Kraig. *Crop Circles*. Minneapolis, Minn.: Bellwether Media, 2011.

Nobleman, Marc Tyler. *Aliens and UFOs*. Chicago, Ill.: Raintree, 2007.

Wencel, Dave. *UFOs*. Minneapolis, Minn.: Bellwether Media, 2010.

ON THE WEB

Learning more about alien abductions is as easy as 1, 2, 3.

1. Go to www.factsurfer.com.

2. Enter "alien abductions" into the search box.

3. Click the "Surf" button and you will see a list of related Web sites.

With factsurfer.com, finding more information is just a click away.

INDEX